TO POO OR NOT TO POO

PHILOSOPHICAL THOUGHTS FROM THE SMALLEST ROOM

TOM BELL

This book is a work of humor and intended for entertainment purposes only.

Published by Sourcebooks, Inc.
P.O. Box 4410, Naperville, Illinois 60567-4410
(630) 961-3900
Fax: (630) 961-2168
www.sourcebooks.com

Originally published as *To Poo or Not to Poo* in 2015 in the United Kingdom by Summersdale Publishers Ltd.

Printed and bound in the United States of America.
WOZ 10 9 8 7 6 5 4 3 2 1

To..

From..

You never know what is
enough unless you know what
is more than enough.

William Blake

You are in the perfect position
to get there from here.

Abraham Hicks

Nothing is more active than thought, and nothing is stronger than necessity, for all must submit to it.

Thales of Miletus

Crocodile dung was used as a contraceptive in ancient Egypt.

———— ————————

To mark their territory, male hippopotamuses defecate while spinning their tails in a propeller motion to ensure it travels a significant distance.

Each forward step
we take we leave
some phantom of
ourselves behind.

John Lancaster Spalding

Pleasure in the job puts perfection in the work.

Aristotle

BY DAILY POOING

I HAVE COME TO BE

Think like a man of action,
act like a man of thought.

Henri Bergson

Each day provides its own gifts.

Marcus Aurelius

There can be no greater rudeness than to interrupt another in the current of his discourse.

John Locke

In World War II, German tank drivers in Africa drove tanks over camel poo for luck. Allied forces responded rather cleverly by planting land mines disguised as camel dung. The Germans got wind of this and instead began riding over camel poo that was already overrun with tank tracks. In turn, the Allies made mines looking like overrun dung.

Fast is fine, but accuracy is everything.

Xenophon

Nothing can have
value without being
an object of utility.

Karl Marx

THE UNEXAMINED POO IS NOT WORTH DOING

No matter where you go or what you do, you live your entire life within the confines of your head.

Terry Josephson

Better a little which is well done, than a great deal imperfectly.

Plato

In a disordered mind,
as in a disordered
body, soundness of
health is impossible.

Cicero

In Japan, many **public toilets** are equipped with a button that can be pressed when necessary to cover up **toilet noises** with the sound of **flushing**.

———————————

In the **early years** of the twentieth century, motor cars were seen as the "green" alternative to **horses**, which were causing major pollution with the **amount of poo** they produced.

Where the willingness is great, the difficulties cannot be great.

Niccolò Machiavelli

Things of this world are in so constant a flux that nothing remains long in the same state.

John Locke

BETTER TO POO AND BE DISAPPOINTED THAN TO NEVER POO AND ALWAYS WONDER

The only Zen you can find
in the small room is the
Zen you bring in there.

Robert M. Pirsig

Make the best use of what
is in your power and take
the rest as it happens.

Epictetus

When you gaze
long into an abyss,
the abyss also
looks into you.

Friedrich Nietzsche

One of the most expensive teas in the world is fertilized with *panda poo*. Pandas only absorb 30 percent of the *nutrients* from their food (bamboo), so their dung is rich in nutrients, which are later absorbed by the *tea plants*.

In all things of nature
there is something
of the marvelous.

Aristotle

Truth is ever to be found in simplicity, and not in the multiplicity and confusion of things.

Isaac Newton

WHEREVER YOU POO, POO WITH ALL YOUR HEART

See without looking, hear without listening, breathe without asking.

W. H. Auden

Good habits formed at youth make all the difference.

Aristotle

Health and
intellect are the two
blessings of life.

Menander

The color of your poo can tell you a great deal about your health. The ideal poo is a brown **continuous log** that sinks to the bottom of the toilet and is **relatively easy** to pass. Different-colored poo can be the result of the food you recently **consumed**. However, if it is obviously not due to food then there is likely to be an underlying **health problem** that needs sorting out.

It is better wither to be silent, or to say things of more value than silence.

Pythagoras

It is easier to do many things than to do one thing continuously for a long time.

Quintilian

I POO, THEREFORE I AM

Consider what each soil will
bear, and what each refuses.

Virgil

It's not what happens to you, but
how you react to it that matters.

Epictetus

silence is one of
the great arts of
conversation.

Cicero

Sloths, the world's laziest animals, poo only once a week, climbing down from their tree to defecate on the ground. Then they cover it up very slowly.

———— — ———

The wombat is unique in the animal kingdom for producing cube-shaped poo. It's said to resemble very pungent dice.

You will find rest
from vain fancies if
you perform every
act in life as though
it were your last.

Marcus Aurelius

Everything has its beauty, but not everyone sees it.

Confucius

HE WHO HAS A PEACEFUL POO DISTURBS NEITHER HIMSELF NOR ANOTHER

Throw moderation to the winds, and the greatest pleasures bring the greatest pains.

Democritus

The sun, too, shines into cesspools and is not polluted.

Diogenes

First say to yourself
what you would be;
and then do what
you have to do.

Epictetus

Contrary to the celebrated story, Thomas Crapper did not invent the flushing toilet. He was, however, a well-known plumber who helped to popularize its use.

—————— ——————

Dried seabird and bat droppings (guano), which consist mainly of potassium nitrate, were once important ingredients in the manufacture of gunpowder.

He is most powerful who
has power over himself.

Seneca the Younger

Commitment is an
act, not a word.

Jean-Paul Sartre

CONTROL THY POO
LEST IT TAKE
VENGEANCE
ON THEE

I attempt an arduous task; but there is no worth in that which is not a difficult achievement.

Ovid

The tighter you squeeze, the less you have.

Zen saying

After a storm comes a calm.

English proverb

The green humphead parrotfish eats coral and poos sand. This has led to the creation of many small islands and sandy beaches in the Caribbean. On average, one parrotfish can produce 90 kg of sand each year.

Criticism comes easier than craftsmanship.

Zeuxis

A multitude of
words is no proof of
a prudent mind.

Thales of Miletus

KNOW THY POO, AND THOU KNOW THYSELF

No one knows what he
can do until he tries.

Publilius Syrus

All things are difficult
before they are easy.

Thomas Fuller

If I have done any deed
worthy of remembrance,
that deed will be my
monument. If not,
no monument can
preserve my memory.

Agesilaus II

Fecal transplants are an effective medical treatment. The procedure is carried out by doctors and involves taking a healthy person's poo and placing it in an unhealthy person's gastrointestinal tract in order to replenish beneficial bacteria in the gut. The treatment has a 90 percent success rate.

———————————

A piece of fossilized poo is known as a coprolite.

The best way to keep good acts in memory is to refresh them with new.

Cato the Elder

Force has no place
where there is
need of skill.

Herodotus

WHERE THERE'S POO,
THERE'S
HOPE

There is nothing so easy but
that it becomes difficult when
you do it reluctantly.

Terence

Never does nature
say one thing and
wisdom another.

Juvenal

What you leave behind
is not what is engraved
in stone monuments,
but what is woven into
the lives of others.

Pericles

Scientists monitor the stress levels of whales by analyzing their poo. This has led to some interesting discoveries. For example, researchers found that some whales were significantly less stressed immediately after the 9/11 attacks because the drop in shipping traffic reduced "acoustic pollution" in the oceans. This noise normally interferes with the low-frequency sounds that whales use to communicate.

True happiness is to enjoy the present without anxious dependence on the future.

Seneca the Younger

Neither blame nor praise yourself.

Plutarch

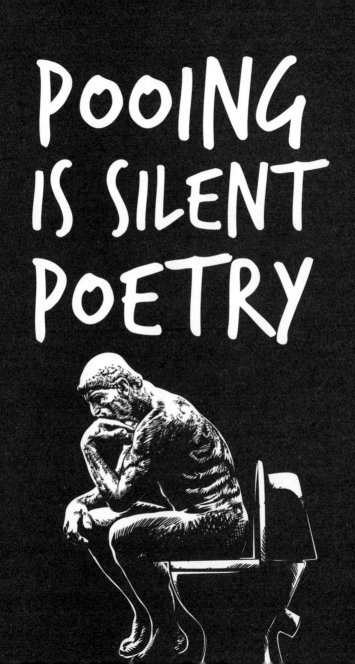

Time brings all things to pass.

Aeschylus

Reading furnishes the
mind only with materials of
knowledge; it is thinking that
makes what we read ours.

John Locke

There are far better
things ahead than
any we leave behind.

C. S. Lewis

Baby elephants, koalas, pandas, and hippos are born without bacteria in their intestines, so they eat the feces of their mothers in order to obtain the bacteria they need to digest vegetation found on the savannah and in the jungle.

———————————————

Ideally, we should poo at least once a day; though some experts say three times a week is sufficient.

Everything in excess is opposed to nature.

Hippocrates

Day by day, what you choose, what you think, and what you do is who you become.

Heraclitus

THE VERY SPRING
AND ROOT OF
HONESTY AND
VIRTUE LIES IN
GOOD POOING

Wisdom begins in wonder.

Socrates

Conceal a flaw, and the world
will imagine the worst.

Martial

Wait for the wisest of all counselors, time.

Pericles

For the first couple of days after a baby is born they produce a dark green or sticky black poo known as meconium. It is made up of the things the baby ingested while in the uterus, such as amniotic fluid and mucus.

———————————

Beaver, Oklahoma, is the undisputed cow dung–flinging capital of the world. It claims to have held the very first "cow chip throwing contest" in 1970.

Difficulties are things that show a person what they are.

Epictetus

Not what we have
but what we enjoy
constitutes our
abundance.

Epicurus

IT IS EASIER TO DO MANY POOS THAN TO DO ONE POO CONTINUOUSLY FOR A LONG TIME

Beauty in things exists in the mind which contemplates them.

David Hume

Beware the barrenness of a busy life.

Socrates

A bad beginning makes a bad ending.

Euripides

One of the most **expensive** coffees in the world, *kopi luwak*, is made from coffee berries that have been eaten and defecated by the *Asian palm civet* (toddy cat). The seeds are collected from their *poo.*

The end of labor is
to gain leisure.

Aristotle

The greater the obstacle, the more glory in overcoming it.

Molière

EVERY POO HAS ITS BEAUTY, BUT NOT EVERYONE SEES IT

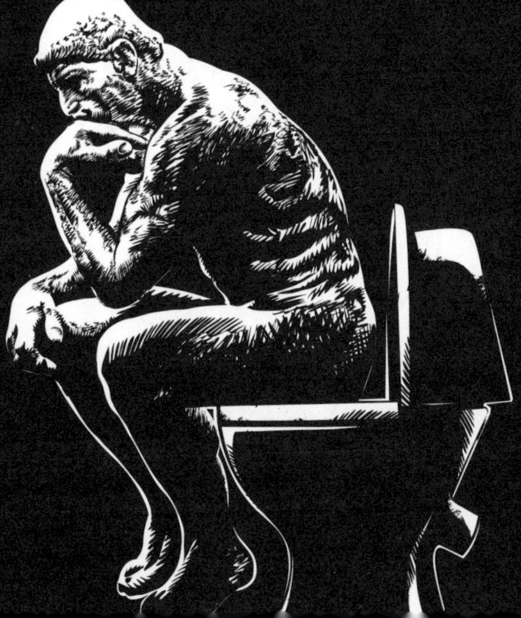

The beginning in every
task is the chief thing.

Plato

The energy of the mind
is the essence of life.

Aristotle

A man's character is his fate.

Heraclitus

When Neil Armstrong's Apollo 11 mission headed back to Earth, they left behind four bags of astronaut poo on the moon.

———————————

According to the Bristol Stool Scale, there are seven different categories or types of poo.

Wisdom comes alone
through suffering.

Aeschylus

What it lies in our power to do, it lies in our power not to do.

Aristotle

POO SPRINGS ETERNAL

There is a foolish corner in the
brain of the wisest man.

Aristotle

Everything existing in the universe
is the fruit of chance and necessity.

Democritus

To find fault is easy; to do better may be difficult.

Plutarch

DNA analysis of dog poo is now used in a number of communities and apartment complexes to identify dogs whose mess hasn't been cleaned up by their owners. The company involved in the process is called PooPrints.

If you do not expect the unexpected you will not find it, for it is not to be reached by search or trail.

Heraclitus

No human thing is of
serious importance.

Plato

IT IS NOT POOING THAT MATTERS, BUT POOING RIGHTLY

Hide our ignorance as we will, an evening of wine soon reveals it.

Heraclitus

No matter what happens, it is within my power to turn it to my advantage.

Epictetus

Give me a lever long enough and a fulcrum on which to place it, and I shall move the world.

Archimedes

A Polish rap artist has commissioned and installed a giant statue of dog doo in a park in the hope that it will encourage his fans to clean up after their pets.

————— ——— ·————

The reason you may sometimes see corn in your poo is because the body finds it hard to digest cellulose, a type of carbohydrate found in the fibrous outer shells of corn kernels.

I was once a skeptic
but was converted by
the two missionaries on
either side of my nose.

Robert Brault

Time is the most
valuable thing a
man can spend.

Theophrastus

POOING IS A SHORT-LIVED TYRANNY

It is easy to stand a pain, but difficult to stand an itch.

Chang Ch'ao

Time flies never to be recalled.

Virgil

Nature does nothing
uselessly.

Aristotle

Guano is the droppings of seabirds and cave-dwelling bats. It is such a highly valued fertilizer that the Incan people used to punish anyone caught disturbing the seabird colonies with death.

———— ——— ————

Poo is made up of 75 percent water and 25 percent solid matter. Roughly a third of the solid matter is dead bacteria that were living in your intestines.

One does what one
is; one becomes
what one does.

Robert Musil

He is richest who is content with the least, for content is the wealth of nature.

Socrates

IF POO
COULD TALK,
WE WOULD NOT
UNDERSTAND IT

Practice yourself in little things,
and thence proceed to greater.

Epictetus

Success is dependent on effort.

Sophocles

Never go to excess,
but let moderation
be your guide.

Cicero

People in south Asia produce three times as much poo as British people due to the higher fiber content of their diet.

————— ·———

The brown coloration of poo comes from dead red blood cells and bile, the fluid secreted into your intestines to help digest fats.

People are not
disturbed by things,
but by the view they
take of them.

Epictetus

Well begun is
half done.

Aristotle

DO NOT SPEAK OF YOUR POO TO ONE LESS FORTUNATE

Men who wish to know about
the world must learn about it
in its particular details.

Heraclitus

Do not consider painful
what is good for you.

Euripides

Not even the gods fight
against necessity.

Simonides of Ceos

On average, a **woman's colon** is about 10 cm longer than a man's. As a result, women can take **a bit longer** to poo than men and they may be more prone to **bloating** and **constipation**.

The secret of happiness
is freedom. The secret
of freedom is courage.

Thucydides

When one is eager
and willing, the
gods join in.

Aeschylus

ALL MEN, BY NATURE, DESIRE TO POO

Whether you think you can or think you can't, you're right.

Henry Ford

As a rule, men worry more about what they can't see than about what they can.

Julius Caesar

Short is the joy that guilty pleasure brings.

Euripides

To be a gold-star pooper you need plenty of plant fiber and gut bacteria. Eat lots of fruit, vegetables, nuts, and seeds; avoid taking antibiotics if possible because they kill off good gut bacteria; and consider taking a probiotic supplement.

Great deeds are usually wrought at great risks.

Herodotus

There is no harm in repeating a good thing.

Plato

IF YOU WISH TO POO, THEN POO

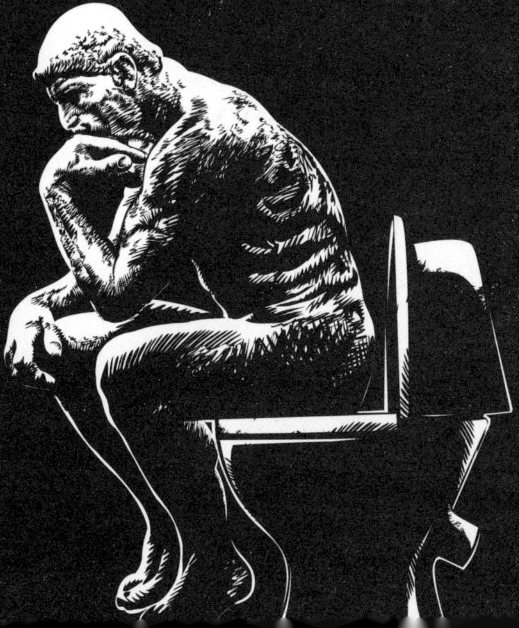

We become just by performing just action, temperate by performing temperate actions, brave by performing brave actions.

Aristotle

As the builders say, the larger stones do not lie well without the lesser.

Plato

Haste in every business
brings failures.

Herodotus

One of the most *effective* ways to improve your bowel movement is to *squat*. Squatting straightens your rectum and relaxes your puborectalis muscle which helps you to empty your bowel *without straining*.

Man is the most
intelligent of
the animals and
the most silly.

Diogenes

There is nothing impossible to him who will try.

Alexander the Great

POOING IS
A KIND OF
SALVATION

The whole is more than
the sum of its parts.

Aristotle

Moderation in all things.

Terence

Small opportunities are often the beginning of great enterprises.

Demosthenes

The pungency of poo varies according to your diet and health. Processed foods and meat can lead to a sluggish digestive system, where waste begins to rot and release foul-smelling gases and stools. Stinky stools can also be a sign of a more serious underlying medical condition, so it's best to go the doctor or see a dietitian if your poo is consistently too pungent.

Anticipate the difficult by managing the easy.

Lao Tzu

The happiness of
your life depends
on the quality of
your thoughts.

Marcus Aurelius

ONE WAY TO GET THE MOST OUT OF POOING IS TO LOOK UPON IT AS AN ADVENTURE

We should not moor a ship with one anchor, or our life with one hope.

Epictetus

Life is really simple, but we insist on making it complicated.

Confucius

Whatever comes from
God is impossible for
a man to turn back.

Herodotus

Undigested seeds can pass through the digestive system and later germinate. Tomato plants can sometimes be seen growing where sewage sludge has been used as fertilizer.

———————————————

Diarrhea is defined as having three or more loose or liquid bowel movements per day. Bowel movements that are infrequent or difficult to pass qualify as constipation, even if they occur on a daily basis.

The excessive increase
in anything causes
a reaction in the
opposite direction.

Plato

No man is hurt
but by himself.

Diogenes

POOING IS NOT A PROBLEM TO BE SOLVED, BUT A REALITY TO BE EXPERIENCED

To do the same thing over and over again is not only boredom: it is to be controlled by rather than to control what you do.

Heraclitus

Toil is no source of shame; idleness is shame.

Hesiod

You'll come to learn
a great deal if you
study the Insignificant
in depth.

Odysseus Elytis

Paleofeces are ancient human poos. They are often discovered during archaeological digs and in caves in arid climates. Analysis of the content of these poos can reveal the diet and health of the people who produced them.

———————————

The "pooper scooper" was invented by a lady in California to help dog owners clear up after their dogs. She holds a patent for a metal bin with a rake-like edge attached to a wooden stick. The generic term pooper scooper was included in the dictionary in the early 1970s.

Blushing is the
color of virtue.

Diogenes

Big results require big ambitions.

Heraclitus

NO MAN EVER DOES THE SAME POO TWICE, FOR IT'S NOT THE SAME POO, AND HE'S NOT THE SAME MAN

We must free ourselves of the hope that the sea will ever rest. We must learn to sail in high winds.

Aristotle Onassis

Men's natures are alike; it is their habits that carry them far apart.

Confucius

The most beautiful and most profound experience is the sensation of the mystical.

Albert Einstein

Different cultures use a variety of "personal cleansing" practices after defecation. In Ancient Rome, a communal sponge was the preferred method. It was rinsed in a bucket of salt water or vinegar between uses.

When checking the safety of water sources and soil, one of the things scientists look out for is the presence of bacteria called *E. coli*, which indicates poo contamination.

All excellent things are as difficult as they are rare.

Baruch Spinoza

If one way be better than another, that you may be sure is nature's way.

Aristotle

THE MONOTONY AND **SOLITUDE** OF A QUIET POO STIMULATES THE CREATIVE MIND

Out of discord comes the fairest harmony.

Heraclitus

Let him that would move the world first move himself.

Socrates

To read without reflecting is like eating without digesting.

Edmund Burke

Rabbits can poo more than 500 pellets a day, some of which they will reingest in order to extract further nutrients.

The average human can produce up to two pounds of poo a day, but that's nothing compared to an African elephant, which can produce up to 300 pounds of dung each day.

Life is not a problem to be solved, but a reality to be experienced.

Søren Kierkegaard

Happiness is when what you think, what you say, and what you do are in harmony.

Mahatma Gandhi

SOME POOS ARE BLESSINGS, SOME POOS ARE LESSONS